BE A MAKER!

MAKER PROJECTS FOR KIDS WHO LOVE

GRAPHIC DESIGN

JAMES BOW

CRABTREE
Publishing Company
www.crabtreebooks.com

Crabtree Publishing Company

www.crabtreebooks.com

Author: James Bow

Publishing plan research and development:
Reagan Miller

Editors: Sarah Eason, Harriet McGregor,
Reagan Miller

Proofreaders: Nancy Dickmann, Petrice Custance

Editorial director: Kathy Middleton

Design: Paul Myerscough

Cover design: Emma DeBanks

Photo research: Rachel Blount

**Production coordinator and
  Prepress techician:** Tammy McGarr

Print coordinator: Margaret Amy Salter

Consultant: Chris Stone

Production coordinated by Calcium Creative

Photo Credits:

t=Top, bl=Bottom Left, br=Bottom Right

Dreamstime: Mike Clegg: p. 7; Brett Critchley: pp. 1, 19; Flickr:
College of DuPage: p. 27; XU Sustainable Sanitation Center/Meiyoshi
Acabal Masgon: p. 5; Freestockphotos.biz: CDC/Amanda Mills: p. 26;
Shutterstock: Dean Bertoncelj: p. 4; Sandratsky Dmitriy: p. 25; File404:
p. 6; Hcreate: p. 12tr; Nito: p. 10; Popartic: p. 18; Serhiy Yermak: p. 12tl;
Tudor Photography: pp. 12–13, 22–23, 28–29; Wikimedia Commons:
Milton Glaser: p. 21; GPL: p. 11; Hay Kranen: p. 13; Mmxx: p. 24–25;
Andrés Nieto Porras: p.25; Tom Photographer: p. 8; Vlasta2: p. 9.

Cover: Tudor Photography.

Library and Archives Canada Cataloguing in Publication

Bow, James, 1972-, author
    Maker projects for kids who love graphic design / James Bow.

(Be a maker!)
Includes index.
Issued in print and electronic formats.
ISBN 978-0-7787-2250-2 (bound).--
ISBN 978-0-7787-2262-5 (paperback).--
ISBN 978-1-4271-1719-9 (html)

        1. Graphic arts--Juvenile literature. I. Title.

NC997.B558 2016   j740   C2015-907924-1
                                                 C2015-907925-X

Library of Congress Cataloging-in-Publication Data

Names: Bow, James, author.
Title: Maker projects for kids who love graphic design / James
    Bow.
Description: New York : Crabtree Publishing Company, 2016.
    | Series: Be a maker! | Includes index. | Description based
    on print version record and CIP data provided by publisher;
    resource not viewed.
Identifiers: LCCN 2015046007 (print) | LCCN 2015045751
    (ebook) | ISBN 9781427117199 (electronic HTML) | ISBN
    9780778722502 (reinforced library binding : alk. paper) | ISBN
    9780778722625 (pbk. : alk. paper)
Subjects: LCSH: Graphic arts--Juvenile literature.
Classification: LCC NC997 (print) | LCC NC997 .B558 2016
    (ebook) | DDC 740--dc23
LC record available at http://lccn.loc.gov/2015046007

Crabtree Publishing Company

www.crabtreebooks.com   1-800-387-7650

Printed in Canada/022016/MA20151130

Published in Canada
Crabtree Publishing
616 Welland Ave.
St. Catharines, Ontario
L2M 5V6

Published in the United States
Crabtree Publishing
PMB 59051
350 Fifth Avenue, 59th Floor
New York, New York 10118

Published in the United Kingdom
Crabtree Publishing
Maritime House
Basin Road North, Hove
BN41 1WR

Published in Australia
Crabtree Publishing
3 Charles Street
Coburg North
VIC, 3058

CONTENTS

TIME TO MAKE!

Do you like to write or draw? Have you spent time coloring things on paper? We all like making things with our hands. What you might not know is how important these skills are. Writing and drawing may seem like playing rather than working, but by using them together you can share your ideas with the world.

HAND TO EYE

Look at the book you are holding. See how the words are placed and how they are shaped. Look at the colors on the pages and where the pictures are. Notice how the letters of some words are shaped differently from others, such as thicker or in different colors. See how these **elements** move your eyes across the page in a certain order.

A lot of people worked very hard to produce the words and pictures you see. They made them in such a way that your eye follows the words, making it easier to understand what they are telling you. The combination of words, colors, and pictures makes this page fun to look at, and that makes the page easier to read. The process that puts all this together is called graphic design.

Superman's logo is simple yet suggests Superman's attributes through the use of colors and lettering.

Be a Maker!

Do you believe that we are controlling where your eyes look on this page? Try reading the parts of this page out of order. How hard is that to do? Look at the page again: what is the first thing you see? What is the first thing you read?

EVERYWHERE A MAKERSPACE

You can use the words you write and the pictures you draw to reach out to people. In fact, by playing with your art and your writing, you are learning how to become a maker.

Makerspaces are places where we unleash our creativity. We play with new ideas and we share what we have made with others. We learn from mistakes and we adapt old ideas to make new things. A makerspace can be in your library, your school, on the Internet, or at home.

By trying the activities in this book, or being inspired by what you read here, you can turn the space around you into a makerspace. Now let's get started!

Group collaboration, or working as a team, is a great makerspace way to create new ideas and improve individual projects.

THE ART OF GRAPHIC DESIGN

Graphic design uses both words and pictures to deliver a message to the reader or viewer. Graphic design **communicates**. Graphic design can express emotions, deliver important information quickly, or help you understand what you are reading.

AROUND THE WORLD

Walk down a street and look at the signs. Pick up a newspaper and look at the articles. Almost everything around you uses graphic design. Signs and maps use graphic design to tell you where you are and where you can go. Books and magazines use graphic design to help readers read their stories. **Advertisements** use graphic design to make you want to buy things.

You may wonder, if there is something people need to know, why not write it down for them? The problem is, not everybody can read, or read in all languages. Even if they can read, they might not have time to read something complicated. You do not want a sign that uses paragraphs of text to tell you how to leave a building if the building is on fire! You want a sign that says "EXIT" and points you to the right door.

Graphic design produced these images that clearly communicate a message without written language.

EASY READING

Even if you have time to read, good graphic design makes reading easier. Well-made books use particular styles of text that are easy to read. Newspapers and magazines use headlines and **subheadings** to summarize stories and break up text into smaller sections. Not only does this **emphasize** the important points of the text, it makes it easier to find that text again when you look for it.

THOUGHTS AND FEELINGS

Pictures and words share information in different ways. Words reach out to our thoughts, while pictures appeal to our emotions. You can use a lot of words to describe a scene, but a picture takes viewers there in an instant. If we want people to think and react emotionally at the same time, we cannot use just text, or just pictures. Both are useful tools, but they are even more powerful when used together.

Advertising uses graphic design to catch the eye and sell you things. However, a lot of different advertising in one place can be overwhelming.

Be a Maker!

Is a picture worth a thousand words? What information has to be communicated quickly? What things can you think of that need to be explained in detail? Would text or pictures be better for these messages, or a combination of both?

GRAPHIC DESIGN THROUGH THE AGES

The first graphic designers lived more than 30,000 years ago! At this time, our ancestors in Europe and Asia started drawing pictures of animals on cave walls. They drew pictures of themselves and the lives they lived.

PICTURES FIRST

We are not sure why people started drawing. Some suggest our ancestors were drawing the animals they hunted as an act of worship. Others suggest people drew pictures to teach others how to hunt. Perhaps they were simply telling people they had been there. Either way, these early drawings communicated a message, and that makes them a form of graphic design. Even before words were written, stories were told through art. In medieval Europe, when most people could not read, the pictures on stained glass windows, or **murals** and paintings like those in the Sistine Chapel in the Vatican, told stories from the Bible.

THE ART OF WRITING

Writing started between 6,000 and 9,000 years ago, in Mesopotamia and China. Words could communicate ideas and instructions in ways that pictures could not. And because most people could not read, writing was something that only rich and educated people could do.

Chinese calligraphers use brushes to write words. Their language uses characters to represent objects and ideas.

In the early years, writing was as much art as language. The ancient Egyptians created a picture language that we know today as **hieroglyphs**. Even when letters were first used instead of pictures, the letters were often stylishly drawn in ink in a process called **calligraphy**.

PRINTING BEGINS

In the past, scholars copied books by hand. It took months to copy an entire book, and it kept writing out of the hands of most people. Around 1440, a German blacksmith named Johannes Gutenberg created a machine called a printing press. He was an innovative maker, and invented a way to make a mold that could cast letters in metal. Gutenberg's presses and the ones that followed could produce 3,600 pages of text a day. Books could be produced in the thousands. They were no longer limited to the rich.

As more people read, ideas spread. Newspapers taught people the idea of democracy, which fueled revolutions in North America and France in the 1700s.

This reconstruction of Gutenberg's famous printing press is found at the International Printing Museum in California.

Be a Maker!

Before the printing press, news was handed out by people who had the time and the money to hand-write and personally deliver the news. After the printing press, people could make and deliver their own newspapers. How do you think this changed the type of news reported?

GOING DIGITAL

As technology improved, printing became faster and easier. English inventor Henry Mill created the first typewriter in 1714. This device pressed metal keys on ink and paper, and helped people write documents that were more **legible** than handwriting.

LITHOGRAPHY

In 1796, a Bavarian actor named Alois Senefelder invented **lithography**. Oil was placed on a smooth stone or metal surface. The oil repelled water, but held on to oil-based ink that could be pressed to paper. A few years later, other inventors built upon this technique to apply different colored inks at different stages in the printing process. This is called offset printing, and it meant that printing could be done in full color.

FASTER AND FASTER

Computers made printing even easier. Ink-jet printers squirt ink, while laser printers use lasers to create a static electric charge that attracts toner (powdered ink) to paper, where a heat roller fuses it into place. However, the first computers could not easily show things like graphics, or even changes to the text that would appear on the printer. Publishers used a markup language that placed symbols around certain words to tell the computer what to do with them. A phrase like bold this text would appear in print as **bold this text**.

As the operator hits a key on a typewriter, an arm moves up toward the paper and stamps the letter on the paper.

WYSIWYG

In the 1980s, new **desktop publishing** software was developed. This WYSIWYG ("what you see is what you get") technology allowed people to see their design on the screen before printing it. This made it easier for makers to publish newsletters or books at home.

More recently, the Internet has meant that people no longer need paper to publish. Websites and blogs, along with online **art portfolio** sites, allow writers, designers, and other makers to reach thousands of viewers with just a few clicks of a mouse.

Desktop publishing programs, such as Scribus, show you what your text and images look like before you print them.

Makers and Shakers

Elizabeth Pickering

Elizabeth Pickering (1510–1562) was the first woman to print books in England. She kept her husband's printing business running after he died, and printed a number of books about law. Women like Pickering also printed things men would not have printed, like books on how to manage a house, fiction novels, and pamphlets about the rights of women. Pickering's works are among the oldest printed books still existing today.

ELEMENTS OF DESIGN

Space is another element that makers use because they must make sure their work is easy to see and understand. They follow principles that you can also follow in your graphic design maker projects.

The geometric shapes are precise and ordered, while the organic shapes are much freer and wild.

SHAPE

Makers need to understand that shapes stand out from the space around them. All of the objects in a design are made up of shapes. Shapes can be geometric (square, circle, or triangle, all drawn by a ruler or a compass) or organic (squiggly lines drawn by hand). Geometric shapes create a sense of control or order, while organic shapes have a more natural feel.

COLOR

Using color makes objects and shapes stand out, and different colors produce different emotions in the people who see them. Warm colors like red, orange, and yellow excite the viewer, while cool colors like green, blue, and purple calm the viewer. Warm colors stand out while cool colors fade into the background.

TEXTURE

Texture describes how a surface feels. Graphic designers can use different paper and materials to affect the actual texture of their designs. They can also use different patterns to create the illusion of texture.

SPACE

Space is another element of design that makers use to make an object stand out. Designs or text that use a lot of white space are easy to see or read, but can look bare. Designs or text that do not have a lot of white space may look interesting and full, but they can also be confusing and hard to read.

FOCAL POINT

The **focal point** is the part of your design to which the eye is drawn. This is not always the center of the picture. In a photograph, the focal point is the part of the picture that is most in focus. In a painting, the focal point might be the brightest part. It is here that you want to put the information that tells your viewers what your design is about, and encourage them to read on.

Makers can create more than one focal point in their design piece. The first focal point you look at is the one that **dominates** the image, by being brighter or more noticeable than the rest.

In this design, the red square jumps out. It is the dominant focal point of this piece. The yellow and blue squares also stand out from the other white squares. Your eye will go to these focal points after you are done looking at the red focal point.

Be a Maker!

How would you turn words into a focal point? How would you shape or color your words to excite people, or calm them down?

TYPEFACES

Words communicate not just by what they say, but how they look. The style of a letter's shape is known as a **typeface**. Thousands of different typefaces exist. Dozens can be found on your computer. Each letter is carefully designed so that readers can join these letters in their mind to form words.

STYLES

Makers create typefaces and the typefaces generally fall into one of four categories: **serif**, sans-serif, script (like handwriting), and decorative. Serif and sans-serif are used most often.

A serif is a small line found at the end of a stroke in a letter. They may date back to Roman carvers who used these to make it easier to chisel letters into stone. Sans-serif typefaces remove these lines, giving the letters a cleaner look. The typeface used in this book is sans-serif.

A novel will likely use serif text inside, as serif typefaces make it easier for readers to read large blocks of text on paper. Sans-serif typefaces are easier to read in small blocks or lines of text, making them useful for signs. It is also easier to read sans-serif typefaces on a screen, which is why most major websites, like Facebook, use sans-serif.

English artist Eric Gill (1882–1940) created some of the most commonly used typefaces seen today, such as Perpetua (top), a serif typeface, and Gill Sans (bottom), a sans-serif typeface.

Eric Gill

Eric Gill

light

light italic

book

book italic

bold

bold italic

The letters above are set in the typeface Garamond. The six styles above show different weights and slopes of the typeface.

WEIGHT OF WORDS

Within typeface families, letters can have different weights. They can be bolded, or made light. Then there is slope, where the letters of a typeface lean forward, like in *italics*. Use of bolding and italics emphasizes words, and conveys a sense of urgency.

Kerning describes the amount of space between letters or words. Kerning not only allows you to fit more text on a single line, it changes the way we think of the words in our mind. Think of how much longer we think the word "longer" is if it is written out as "l o n g e r." Overuse these elements, however, and you can make text hard to read.

Be a Maker!

What kind of typeface would you use to advertise a concert? Would you use bolding or italics on a poster listing the rules at your school, or warning people to avoid a dangerous area? Share your ideas with your friends. Collaboration is key to being a maker.

MAKE IT!
CREATE A WORD CLOUD

We can now put our knowledge of design elements and typefaces to use by creating a **word cloud**. A word cloud is an image composed of words that relate to each other in some way. The size of each word shows you how important it is. With a word cloud, you can describe a story, make a statement, or, as shown below, you could make your word cloud about yourself.

YOU WILL NEED
- A pad of paper
- A pencil and pens
- Pencil crayons and markers

1
- Think about who you are, and how you would describe yourself.
- On a sheet of paper, sketch some images or shapes that you might like your word cloud to form. Perhaps the shape is the form of something that is important to your subject.
- Next, on a new sheet of paper, make a list of words that are important to your subject.

2
- Choose which image you are going to use and write down the most important word in large, bold letters in any style that you like. As the subject of this word cloud is you, this may be your name. Feel free to use color.

3

- Write the other words in your list around your main word, with more important words being larger, and less important words smaller.
- Arrange the words in interesting ways, and build up the shape of the cloud. Try it a few different ways, until you are happy with it.
- Color your design.

- Once you have added all of your words, **embellish** it and display your word cloud proudly.

4

CONCLUSION

Look at the words in your word cloud. Do the shapes of the words match the message they are sending? How do the positions of the words affect each other? What would happen if you moved the words, or drew them differently?

Make It Even Better!

How else can you change your word cloud? Could you alter the alignment of words, running them vertically or diagonally, instead of horizontally? You can also make word clouds online. Do a search for "word cloud" on the Internet.

HIERARCHY

In a design with more than one focal point, a maker must decide which focal point should be "in charge" of the rest. Just as there is a chain of command in an army, how you decide which focal points dominate is called **hierarchy**. The first focal point dominates the rest by being brighter, larger, or surrounded by more white space. You can change which focal point dominates by changing its color, shape, and space.

STAND OUT

Look at the cover of a magazine. Which stories do you look at first? Chances are, you look at the headline with the largest text. You may also look at a story placed next to a big color picture. Then your eyes pick out the smaller headlines on the page, highlighting other stories.

The people who make magazines use hierarchy to show what they think are the most important stories. Hierarchy is also used in writing newspaper stories: the section at the top answers the important questions of who, what, where, when, and why. The next section tells you important details in greater depth, while the rest of the article finishes off with general or background information.

Using the position of the text as a clue, ask yourself what is the magazine's name? What is the most important article? Who or what is profiled on the cover?

MOVIE AND CONCERT POSTERS

You see hierarchy on all graphic designs. Movie posters will usually have the title of the movie as the largest text on the page. Other details, like who is starring in the movie, or when the movie will premiere, are smaller. Posters for a concert will similarly emphasize who is playing by printing names larger. More popular singers will be printed in larger text than less popular supporting acts.

It may seem unfair to promote one star over another, and in design you may be tempted to highlight as many important details as you can. This can create a mess that people have difficulty reading. Hierarchy exists because you cannot emphasize everything. You have to pick the details that are most important and get them to the viewer first.

Each ad here must work to stand out from the rest. It must communicate its message quickly before your eye moves on.

Be a Maker!

What are the most important details you want to get to a viewer when promoting a concert? Would this be different for a poster promoting a political rally?

IDEAS IN PICTURES

While words communicate in detail, people react to a picture instantly. As a result, makers and designers often use **pictographs** to give out information. A pictograph is a symbol that communicates the meaning of a word or phrase.

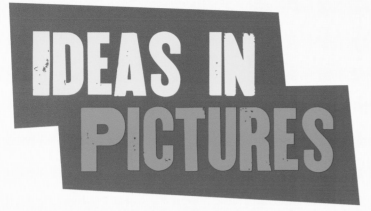

exit

stop —

— no cell phones

SYMBOLS

Pictographs are used a lot on maps. A cross symbol is often used to mark churches, while a symbol with a flat line, with short lines, like reeds, sticking up shows a swamp or a marsh. Some symbols look like the things they represent, which helps you understand what the symbols mean.

These symbols and signs are easily recognized all around the world. The pictographs instantly communicate their information.

INCLUSIVE DESIGN

Pictographs convey information to anyone who cannot understand the local language. Road signs use pictures to warn about hazards ahead, like narrow bridges, falling rocks, or railroad crossings. Some designs work better than others, and many have been changed as improvements are discovered. Until recently, most signs showing a building's exit featured the word "EXIT" in red letters. Today, in some countries, many of these signs are green, showing a picture of a person running through a doorway.

LOGOS

Another way people communicate with pictures is by using logos. Companies use logos to represent their organization and identify their products or services. In the past, logos were text-heavy signs, but today they involve fewer words and more abstract shapes. The goal of a good logo is to be recognized at a glance, or from a distance. Advertising connects the logo to the product, so that when you see the golden arches of McDonald's, you know there are burgers for sale. Logo designers are true makers—they often take risks in their design, and will revisit a design over and over, improving it until they and the company they work for are happy.

The "I ♥ New York" logo uses an American Typewriter typeface to convey an image of a hard-working American city.

I ♥ NY ®

Makers and Shakers

Milton Glaser

American designer Milton Glaser (born 1929) produced dozens of posters throughout his career. His most famous work came in 1977 when he created the "I ♥ NY" logo for an advertising campaign promoting tourism in New York City. Glaser's simple logo took off. The campaign it backed is credited for helping turn around New York City's rough reputation.

MAKE IT!
CREATE A LOGO

Now that we know the importance of color, shapes, and symbols, as well as words, we can put our skills to use by designing a logo. Remember that a logo is usually very simple in design. Your logo should be easy for others to understand, even when seen from a distance.

YOU WILL NEED
- Pencil and eraser
- Pencil crayons or markers
- A pad of paper
- Ruler (optional)
- Compass (optional)

1

- Research logos that you think work well. Create a **design brief**, or a detailed plan to help create your logo. Your design plan should answer the following questions:
  - What will your logo represent?
  - What does your logo advertise?
  - Who do you want to see it?
  - What message will it convey?

- Start brainstorming and sketching, putting your ideas down on paper in a series of **thumbnail sketches**.
- After brainstorming, review your sketches and choose your strongest options.
- Redraw and refine these sketches to create a few **prototypes**. A prototype is an original design.

2

22

3

- Show your prototypes to your friends and ask for feedback.
- You can ask them questions about your choice of colors, use of space, and symbols.
- You can ask what message each logo prototype conveys.
- On a new piece of paper, revise your preferred logo according to the best of your friends' feedback and your own ideas.

- Once you have made your changes and feel confident about the design, you can create a final version of your logo.
- Make it the best quality possible.
- Present it to your friends and start to spread your message through your logo.

4

Make It Even Better!

How many logos can you see when you are out? How many can you see close up? How many can you see far away? How do these logos use color, weight, shape, and texture to make sure you can see them even when you are farther away? Can you apply these techniques to your logo?

CONCLUSION

Take a critical look at your logo. Is it easy to read, even at a distance? What does it tell others about you, or what you do?

RESHAPING THE WORLD

Just as desktop publishing software and printers make it easier for us to create magazines and posters, graphics software and scanners have helped artists make pictures electronically. Computers also give makers the ability to easily **edit** and change their works.

REAL OR FAKE?

Changing photographs used to be a complicated process of drawing, cutting, and pasting. Today, graphics software give individuals a great deal of power to change photographs or create scenes. People have become so good at creating images that look real—but are not—that a word was coined based on the name of one of those programs. Such pictures are said to be "Photoshopped."

Many pictures seen today in magazines are altered. Famous people have blemishes brushed over. Poles are removed from street scenes if they distract from the picture. Other things are added to pictures to show how they would look in the real world, like a proposed skyscraper being added to a skyline. Others change photographs to make funny jokes.

Be a Maker!

Can you think of ways that could help you tell if a photo is real or fake? When is it sometimes hard to tell real from fake? Do you think changing an image is ever the right thing to do?

Computer software packages allow you to build images of the world that are not possible in reality. Which parts of this photograph do you think have been edited?

CHANGING HISTORY

People have been changing photographs to change history for decades. In the 1930s, the Communist Party released a picture of the leader of the Soviet Union, Joseph Stalin, on a boat with party officials including an officer named Nikolai Yezhov. A couple of years later, Yezhov fell out of favor with Stalin, and was executed. Stalin ordered Yezhov's name erased from all records. The photograph of Yezhov standing next to Stalin was altered to make it look as though Yezhov was never there.

CRITICISM

With photo editing tools on computers, you can cut images (called cropping) to focus the picture on the elements you want to show. You may want to show a person playing in a field, leaving out parts that are less important to the picture, such as a big stretch of sky. Programs can take parts of the background and copy it over something in the foreground, removing signs or poles that are blocking the main elements of the picture. You have a lot of power with photo editing programs. Be sure to use it for good!

This picture of Mont Saint-Michel has been photoshopped to add the water and the reflection.

BE A MAKER IN GRAPHIC DESIGN

Graphic designers are not born knowing how to do graphic design. They learn by playing with words and pictures, by looking at what others have done, and incorporating different techniques into their own designs. They make mistakes and learn from them. They share their ideas with others, and act on good suggestions received from others. The field of graphic design has changed and grown over time, not just because new technologies have appeared, but because graphic designers look at what has come before, adopt what works best, and try out ideas about what might work better.

MAKE YOUR WORLD A MAKERSPACE

If you like to draw, and if you like to make things with words and images, you are on your way to becoming a maker in the field of graphic design. Start drawing more. Try new things, like using different colors, and working with new tools such as different pencils and inks. Learn how to use graphic design computer programs. Take art classes. See if there is a makerspace where you can share ideas, resources, and knowledge with others. Get and give feedback. Do not take it personally if people criticize your work; part of becoming a maker is learning from mistakes.

A maker learns by seeing what others have done. Research what has been created before, to help spark ideas for new projects.

GET MAKING

Finally, when you are ready, put what you have learned to good use. Volunteer to do graphic design for your school, such as making a poster to advertise a school play. Make a newspaper or magazine for you and your friends. Just as graphic design has grown from cave paintings to web pages, we grow, learn, and improve by experimenting, playing, and sharing with others. Go out there and be a maker!

Keep a portfolio of your work to show others, and also to remind yourself of what you have done.

Makers and Shakers

Paula Scher

Graphic designer and innovative maker Paula Scher was born in 1948. She drew throughout her childhood and went on to study Fine Arts at the Tyler School of Art in Philadelphia. She moved to New York City where she took a number of jobs in advertising and **marketing** departments. She won awards working at CBS Records, designing album cover art. She did not stay with records, though, and branched out into designing signs, book covers, logos, and posters. Some of her most famous works include the Windows 8 logo, and the official 2012 Sundance Film Festival Poster.

MAKE IT!
CREATE YOUR OWN
BUSINESS CARD

Use your new graphic design skills to make a business card. Business cards are designed for different purposes, but many include a logo and a description of the business or person. The card does not have to be for an actual business. You could simply communicate what you want to say about yourself to the people you meet.

● Research the subject of your business card. Create a design brief to answer the following questions:
- What do you want your card to say?
- Is your card going to be about your hobbies, interests, your family, or a club to which you belong?

1

2

● Create thumbnail sketches of how you want your business card to look.
- Where will you put the logo?
- Where will the information go?
- How big should the text be?
- Can you communicate your message simply and quickly?

28

3 Review your sketches alone and with friends, and select a few that you like. Refine your ideas until you have a final design you are happy with.

4 You can draw your business card directly onto cardboard and cut it out, but if you want to mass-produce your card, you will need to design your card using a word processing or graphic software program. You can use a computer printer to print multiple copies of your card.

WINNERS
Running Club

Make It Even Better!

Did you use both sides of your business card? What kinds of information can you put on the back of the business card? How would they be different from what you put on the front of your business card?

CONCLUSION

By using the principles you have learned in this book, you can communicate ideas quickly and effectively. You can sell products, change minds, and make people interested about things.
Use your power wisely!

GLOSSARY

advertisements Displays of various types that sell a product or a service

art portfolio A collection of an artist's best work

calligraphy The art of producing fancy text with a pen or a brush

communicates Shares information

design brief A detailed plan of what you are going to make

desktop publishing Creation of publications on a personal computer

dominates Stands out by being bigger or by looking more important than the things around it

edit To change something, correcting mistakes or making it better or shorter

elements Individual objects or pieces within a group

embellish To make something look more important by adding extra designs or details

emphasize To make something stand out more than the things around it

focal point The part of something that you notice first; something that everything else relates to

hierarchy A way a design is organized, where certain words or images are given more emphasis than others

hieroglyphs Pictures representing words or sounds

kerning The spacing between the letters in a block of text

legible Clear enough for people to see and understand

lithography A printing process that uses oil on a flat stone or metal surface to attract ink to certain parts of the design

makerspaces Places where makers gather to innovate, share resources, and learn from one another

marketing Promoting or selling a product or service to people, usually through advertising

murals Pieces of art usually painted directly onto walls or other large areas

pictographs Symbols that represent a word or a phrase

prototypes The first versions of your designs, which can be developed and improved

serif A small line that sticks out from a stroke of a letter

subheadings Headings that are smaller than headlines, but larger than most text in the book or article. Subheadings introduce a block of text beneath

thumbnail sketches Small, rough drawings made quickly

typeface The design of a set of letters and symbols

word cloud A design that arranges different but related words to visually describe a topic

LEARNING MORE

BOOKS

Kidd, Chip. *Go: A Kidd's Guide to Graphic Design*. Workman, 2013.

Pease, Pamela. *Design Dossier: The World of Design*. Paintbox, 2009.

Pease, Pamela. *Graphic Design for Kids*. Paintbox, 2010.

Roslund, Samantha, and Emily Puckett Rodgers. *Makerspaces*. Cherry Lake, 2013.

Siegfried, René, and Joel Mann. *The Serif Fairy: Explorations in the World of Letters*. Mark Batty, 2007.

WEBSITES

Find lessons and fun projects for kids of all ages wanting to learn more about art and how to make it at:
artforkidshub.com

Discover color, the science behind it, and how it affects us at:
www.colormatters.com

Learn about all aspects of graphic design, try different graphic design projects, and read about the lives of famous and interesting designers at:
www.kidsthinkdesign.org/graphics/index.html

Find a series of online courses for kids and teens to learn about graphic design tools, including programs like Photoshop, at:
www.techrocket.com/graphic-design

INDEX